GW00361876

Wildflowers of Western Australia

NEW
HOLLAND

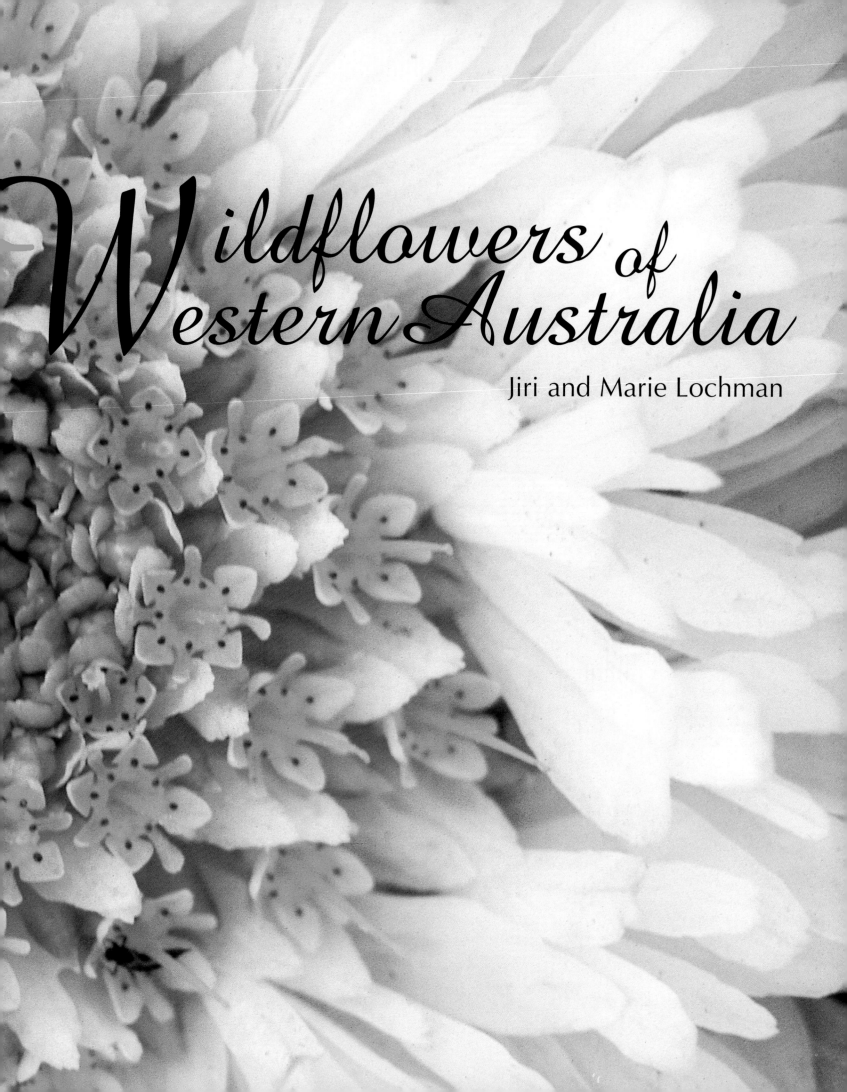

Wildflowers of Western Australia

Jiri and Marie Lochman

First published in Australia in 1998 by
New Holland Publishers (Australia) Pty Ltd
Sydney • Auckland • London • Cape Town

Produced and published in Australia by
New Holland Publishers (Australia) Pty Ltd
14 Aquatic Drive Frenchs Forest NSW 2086 Australia
Unit 1A, 278 Lake Road Northcote Auckland New Zealand
24 Nutford Place London W1H 6DQ United Kingdom
80 McKenzie Street Cape Town 8001 South Africa

Copyright © 1998 in photographs: Jiri and Marie Lochman
Copyright © 1998 in text: Jiri and Marie Lochman
Copyright © 1998 in maps: New Holland Publishers (Australia) Pty Ltd
Copyright © 1998 New Holland Publishers (Australia) Pty Ltd

All rights reserved. No part of this publication may be reproduced,
stored in a retrieval system or transmitted, in any form or by any means,
electronic, mechanical, photocopying, recording or otherwise, without
the prior written permission of the publishers and copyright holders.

National Library of Australia Cataloguing-in-Publication Data:

Lochman, Jiri and Lochman, Marie.
Wildflowers of Western Australia.
Includes index.
ISBN 1 86436 328 2.
1. Wildflowers - Western Australia - Pictorial works. I. Lochman,
Marie. II. Title.

582.1309941

Publishing General Manager: Jane Hazell
Publisher: Averill Chase
Editor: Anna Sanders
Designer: Lyndall du Toit
Map Artwork: Annette Busse
Reproduction: Hirt and Carter Cape (Pty) Ltd
Printer: Tien Wah Press (Pte) Limited, Singapore

HALF TITLE *Devil's Pins* TITLE *Albany Swamp Daisy*
THIS PAGE BELOW *Claw Featherflower* RIGHT *Winter Donkey
Orchid* FAR RIGHT *Everlasting Daisy*

CONTENTS

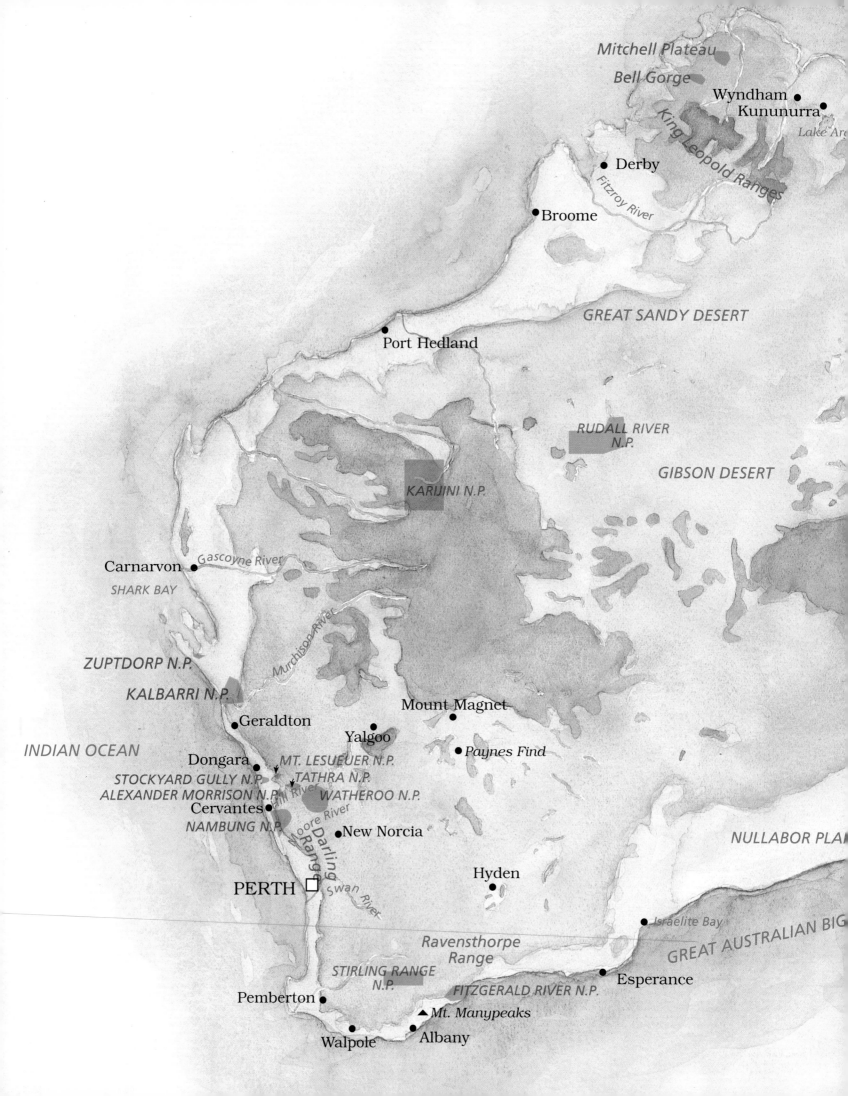

Mitchell Plateau

Bell Gorge

● Wyndham
Kununurra ●

Lake Arg

King Leopold Ranges

● Derby

Fitzroy River

● Broome

GREAT SANDY DESERT

● Port Hedland

RUDALL RIVER N.P.

GIBSON DESERT

KARIJINI N.P.

Gascoyne River

Carnarvon ●

SHARK BAY

Murchison River

ZUPTDORP N.P.

KALBARRI N.P.

Mount Magnet ●

● Geraldton

Yalgoo ●

INDIAN OCEAN

● Paynes Find

Dongara ●

MT. LESUEUER N.P.

STOCKYARD GULLY N.P.

TATHRA N.P.

ALEXANDER MORRISON N.P.

WATHEROO N.P.

Cervantes ●

NAMBUNG N.P.

● New Norcia

NULLABOR PLA

Darling Range

Moore River

PERTH □

Swan River

Hyden ●

● *Israelite Bay*

Ravensthorpe Range

GREAT AUSTRALIAN BIG

STIRLING RANGE N.P.

FITZGERALD RIVER N.P.

● Esperance

Pemberton ●

▲ *Mt. Manypeaks*

Walpole ●

Albany ●

Introduction

The weather in Perth, in the second half of August, when winter is past its peak, can be absolutely delightful. True, nights are still rather cold, just a few degrees above zero, but daytime temperatures rise to a pleasant 20°C. On sunny mornings the air is clear and crisp. This is the most photogenic time of year in Perth. It is also the best time for visiting the southern half of Western Australia, as summers can be too hot and dry, while earlier in winter the weather is unpredictable and unpleasantly wet and cold. Fortunately the change to bright sunny days also coincides with the beginning of the famous West Australian wildflower season.

At this time of year, provided sufficient rain has fallen in the previous few months, the whole landscape some 450 kilometres north-east of Perth, in the region commonly known as the Mid West, becomes carpeted with millions of everlasting and soft daisies, velleias, dampieras, parakeelyas, mulla mullas and other annuals. On opening the doors of an airconditioned vehicle, it is stunning to find the whole region perfumed by a very pleasant, sweet-smelling scent. Smelling an individual flower may bring disappointment however, as its aroma is more often than not too faint for our crude olfactory organs. But no matter how subtle, when multiplied by millions, there is enough fragrance to perfume the entire Mid West.

The northern heathlands further west also come to life at this time of year. Although the flowering season here never ends, the close of winter is the time when it really begins. The yellow wattles are the first to proclaim the arrival of spring in a big way, but other plants blossom before them — several species of banksias, grevilleas, myrtles, pea flowers and a few members of the Australian heath family. As the season progresses more and more species come into bloom here, with the peak around the middle of September.

Towards the end of August, the understorey and ground cover in the forests of the Darling Scarp and the Swan River coastal plain also become adorned by a myriad of flowers. Wattles, growing here in great profusion, are accompanied by hakeas, Bull banksias, petrophiles, lechenaultias, grevilleas and by the Western Australian floral emblem — Red and Green Kangaroo Paws.

The further south one travels, the later the flowering season begins. It also ends later, so it is possible to spend an entire spring following the wildflowers southwards and then eastwards. By December there are still plenty of wildflowers in the heathlands along the south coast, east of Esperance.

BELOW In a good year, thousands of square kilometres in the Mid West region are carpeted by millions of annuals.

When travelling through the south-west of Western Australia it is possible, in theory, to encounter more than 4000 species of flowering plants, or more than one-fifth of the Australian total. However, what is even more staggering is that between 70 and 80 per cent of them are endemic — they do not occur in the wild anywhere else in the world.

It is well known that Western Australia has one of the richest floras in Australia, and the world. With the biggest area and latitudinal distance of all the Australian states, accompanied by a variety of climates, it would seem only natural to assume that Western Australia would have more variety of plant life than the other states. The reality, however, is subtler, and far more surprising, than that. If we draw an imaginary line from Shark Bay in the north to about 100 kilometres east of Esperance, all of the land west of this line is where most of Western Australia's incredible biodiversity occurs — an area not much bigger than the state of Victoria.

ABOVE Southern Kwongan is composed of a myriad mainly woody plants.

The rest of Western Australia would also fare well in comparison with other Australian states in terms of the total number of plant species, but not so much in the number of endemic plants. The majority of West Australian semi-arid and desert plants occur in similar environments in adjoining states. Most of the plant species of the tropical north of Western Australia also extend into the other states, and many of these are also present in tropical Asia or in the Papuan archipelago. Some are even pantropical in their distribution, occurring more or less throughout the tropical regions of the world.

Even within the south-west of the state one finds some environments that contain a markedly greater variety of plants. Some of the richest plant communities in the world can be found here in the heathlands. Known also by their Aboriginal name of Kwongan, they consist mainly of shrubby plants and are formed by a great number of species living close together. Moreover, they differ from area to area in composition, with no two localities being exactly the same.

The occurrence of such a perplexing biodiversity of plants puzzled botanists for a long time: the sandy soils on which these rich heathlands thrive and produce the most spectacular flower displays seem an unlikely source of such a remarkable evolutionary success.

These soils were formed by weathering down of the granitic foundation rocks some 40 to 50 million years ago, when the weather in Western Australia was much wetter and more reminiscent of today's tropics. Because of the great antiquity of these life-bearing top layers of earth and the extraordinary geological stability of the region (which meant that nothing has been added to the soil by subsequent geological upheavals), most nutrients have been leached out, resulting in considerable impoverishment of the soil.

Until recently, it was believed that biodiversity should be greatest in the most nutrient-rich environments. Yet there are ample examples, including coral reefs, tropical rainforests and the West Australian heathlands, which clearly defy such a notion. In all these environments nutrients are in short supply yet a great variety of species flourish. Is it possible then that the opposite might in fact be true?

David Tilman of the University of Minnesota proposes that in environments where essential nutrients such as nitrates and phosphates are in unlimited supply, the species (for which he uses the term 'superspecies') that is best at utilising them can outcompete all similar species. Meanwhile, in resource-poor environments, such as the West Australian heathlands, the subtlest differences in nutrient levels, combined with other variables such as water availability, create a mosaic of dissimilar living spaces. These niches enable the evolution of a great diversity of specialist plants or animals adapted for exploiting them. This, of course, can happen only when geological and climatic stability persists for long enough, as has happened in south-western Australia. The result is today's myriad plants, often closely related, happily coexisting in one of the most deprived environments on Earth where no known superspecies would be able to survive.

Fossil records confirm the assumption that the West Australian wildflower spectacle evolved over a very long time in an almost unchanging environment. This environmental stability ended abruptly some 40 000 years ago with the arrival of the first human colonists, who made big changes with their unsurpassed artistry in environmental exploitation. Though we will never know exactly the impact of fire-stick hunting and large-scale burning on the native flora, we know that following the arrival of Aboriginal Australians, many species that were not fire tolerant either disappeared or began to contract in their range.

An even more consequential event was the second wave of human migration to Australia 200 years ago. Where Aboriginal hunter-gatherers provided for a band of close relatives, Europeans, driven by a profit-making economy, aimed at feeding thousands. Equipped with ever more sophisticated technology for environmental exploitation, farmers have cleared huge tracts of land for large-scale farming. In addition, enticed by successive governments' tax incentives, farmers who may have otherwise restricted their activities to prime productive land completely cleared all original vegetation. Thus, in many cases, not even marginal lands have been spared.

Wholesale land clearing was only one form of attack on the native flora. It was accompanied by the introduction of exotic weeds that proved to be a formidable competing force, especially in disturbed areas. At the same time, the rapidly dwindling undisturbed areas were under pressure from introduced pests such as rabbits and goats.

Furthermore, the destruction of original vegetation cover caused the underground water table to rise and the ensuing rise in salinity still continues to lay waste immense areas of land. The worst affected area was the West Australian wheatbelt region, where estimates suggest that close to 30 per cent of plant species became extinct before they were scientifically recognised.

Fortunately, not all is doom and gloom. A great deal of floral biodiversity remains and we are slowly learning to appreciate the uniqueness of West Australian plants. Simultaneously, we are learning how to mend our ways. Farmers are replanting around 20 000 trees annually to lower the water table and some farmers are adopting more environmentally friendly farming methods. One wheatbelt farmer recently said that he doubts whether his grandfather would have cleared all his land for a tax incentive had he anticipated how expensive his grandson's repayments would be.

A large number of nature reserves have been set aside for the protection of Western Australia's flora. It is up to all of us to look after them and not simply leave it to our professional land managers. The best contribution we can make is to accept our own responsibility; by not picking the flowers; by not moving them for photographs; by accepting that the wellbeing of the object of our passion is more important than our pictures or our momentary admiration; by thinking about what we might destroy before turning our vehicle off the road; by not treating the natural world as something dispensable. The next best contribution we can make is to encourage others to do the same!

LEFT Devastation caused by salinity — formerly a freshwater lake, now saline after indiscriminate removal of vegetation that once covered the area.

The story of wildflowers in Western Australia does not, however, end with plants. For those curious enough to look beyond the obvious, the incredible diversity of West Australian plant life is matched by that of the pollinators who have co-evolved with their hosts. It is not a coincidence, for example, that the only terrestrial equivalent of South American hummingbirds have evolved in the south-west of Western Australia. The honey possum is the only terrestrial mammal in the world that depends solely on nectar and pollen for its sustenance. Unlike birds or bats, this earth-bound nectar feeder cannot fly to faraway places in search of food — it has to be able to find it within its territory. Only here in the south-west of Western Australia is it able to find an almost uninterrupted supply of blossoms throughout the year on just 40 square metres of land.

I hope that, in common with the honey possum, you will be able to find immense joy when looking for wildflowers, even in a small area, and that this book will help you to appreciate the magnificence of West Australian wildflowers.

BELOW This Honey Possum, feeding on a Hooker's Banksia, depends solely on flower blossoms for its existence.

ABOVE Most flowering plants depend on native insects for their procreation — here an Owl Moth feeds on a myrtle flower.

Names for Plants

When discussing species of plants it is necessary to categorise them in some way. It is all very well to enjoy the plants for their beauty, but so much more can be gained by understanding their relationships to each other — the only way to do this is to understand their place in the botanical order. This book has therefore adopted the system used by botanists and plant enthusiasts from all around the world.

In the early 1700s the Swedish zoologist Carl von Linne developed a system for the methodical naming of animals. It used two-word names for every recognised creature and was later adopted by other branches of science, namely botany and medicine. Called the binominal system (meaning consisting of two names) it is still used today. Most of the organisms known to science have been thus scientifically named, usually according to their characteristics. The names are conventionally in Latin or Greek because these were then the languages of scholars of the Western world. By adhering to their use today, scientists ensure that species are always called by the same name regardless of the native language of the scientist.

The first word is the 'generic' name, or genus; it identifies a group of plants that are closely related. For example in the genus *Acacia* there are over 400 different species of plants (Wattles) found in Western Australia alone. The second word denotes the 'species' name, for example *Acacia tropica*, where *tropica* indicates that this particular species occurs in the tropics. All plants with the same two names belong to the same species — in theory they are so closely related that

they should be able to freely interbreed to produce fertile offspring. 'Family' is a higher category into which closely related genera are then placed.

Familiarity with this system provides immediate knowledge; for example, any two plants with the same first name are so closely related that they share certain characteristics. However, another valid reason for using scientific names is the fact that out of 10 000 or so plants occurring in Western Australia less than 10 per cent have acquired a common name.

An advantage of common names is that they can be immediately understood and related to by non-specialist wildflower enthusiasts. While botanical names are often based on minute anatomical features discernible only under a microscope, common names usually refer to the most obvious ones. A flower reminds us of an animal paw, so we call it a kangaroo paw, a ground-covering creeper has s-shaped stems so it is called a snakebush. If such a name is fitting and used for a long enough time it will become widely accepted.

However, common names also have some disadvantages. While no-one can come up with a new scientific name for an already described species, there is no protocol in place regulating the formation of common names, so anyone can invent a new name for any plant, even one with an already established name. This frequently results in confusion as a number of common names may be in usage for a single species, or the same name may be applied to two or more — often unrelated or only superficially similar — plants.

Andersonia caerulea

The Mid West

Any mention of West Australian wildflowers inevitably evokes a picture of vast expanses covered by ever-lasting daisies. Though found in other parts of the state, it is the Mid West region that offers the best displays of these annuals. In a triangle formed roughly by the towns of Mount Magnet, Yalgoo and Paynes Find is the heartland of Western Australia's ephemerals. These carpets of wildflowers are short-lived, being an essentially springtime phenomenon. A visit to the same area in summer would yield only scattered bushes growing from bare, red ground.

In comparison with other plant communities of the Mid West, the fragile beauty of wildflower carpets is composed of relatively few species. Although the everlasting daisies are the most numerous and consequently the best known, other species include Pink Velleias, Cut-leaf Goodenias, several mulla mullas, several species of soft daisies and Parakeelyas.

Further west, in a 150-kilometre wide belt along the coast, are the heathlands that are florally much richer than the colourful carpets of annuals. Unfortunately large areas of these heathlands have succumbed to our demand for arable land. What remains is largely protected by a chain of national parks and nature reserves stretching from Moore River, 120 kilometres north of Perth, to Zuytdorp National Park, some 600 kilometres further north. In between there are many equally important national parks such as Watheroo, Tathra, Alexander Morisson, Lesueur, Stockyard Gully and Nambung. The last-mentioned park is, of course, better known for the peculiar limestone Pinnacles than for its wildflowers.

Kalbarri National Park, the largest in the area, is an easy day's drive along the highway from Perth. It is famous for its spectacular scenery — with over 80 kilometres of deep, craggy gorges, carved by the Murchison River zigzagging through the plains, and by rugged coastal cliffs battered incessantly by the Indian Ocean.

In springtime the main attraction of the Kalbarri National Park lies above the gorges and on top of the cliffs in a vast sandplain covered by a multitude of mainly shrubby plants. There is plenty to see! In early spring, yellow wattles are overwhelming, as are banksias, grevilleas, hakeas, smokebushes, lambstails and cottonheads. Within the borders of this national park 855 species of flowering plants have been recorded, of which 21 do not occur anywhere else!

▲ *Rhodanthe chlorocephala*

ABOVE Pink Everlastings are widespread in the Mid West.
OPPOSITE Floral carpets are formed by a variety of annuals — Pink Cluster Everlasting (dark pink), Pom Pom Everlasting (white), Cut-leaf Goodenia (yellow) and Pink Velleia (light pink).

LEFT AND BELOW Pink Velleia is one of 14 species of velleias found in Western Australia. Thousands of individual plants make up such scenes as the one to the left, taken near Yalgoo.

▲ *Velleia rosea*

▲ *Lechenaultia macrantha*

LEFT AND ABOVE Forming wreath-like rings about half a metre in diameter, the Wreath Lechenaultia usually grows on completely bare ground. The wreath image is enhanced by the fact that the green, needle-like leaves fill the centre while the outward facing flowers grow on the periphery of the ring.

▲ *Calandrinia polyandra*

▲ *Calandrinia granulifera*

TOP AND RIGHT Common Parakeelya can be found in small groups of several plants, or it can form carpets close to water or in places that are seasonally inundated.

ABOVE As with other members of its genus, this minute Parakeelya is a succulent plant; its juice-filled leaves are an important food item for newly hatched emu chicks.

RIGHT   The Umbrella Wattle is an incredibly showy plant when in the peak of its bloom. It is widespread throughout the drier parts of Western Australia.

BELOW   Acacia is the largest genus of plants in Western Australia, comprising some 450 species known collectively as wattles.

BOTTOM   Raspberry Jam is a small tree growing to nine metres. Its freshly cut timber gives the pleasant smell which gave it its common name.

▲ *Acacia sp.*

▲ *Acacia acuminata*

▲ *Acacia ligulata*

▲ *Diplolaena grandiflora*

▲ *Eremophila sp.*

TOP Shark Bay Rose is not related to true roses, but to citrus trees. The Shark Bay Rose has recently risen from obscurity as a plant symbolising the Shark Bay World Heritage Area.

ABOVE About 125 species of woody plants commonly known as Poverty Bushes or Native Fuchsias can be found in Western Australia.

LEFT Coastal dunes in the Zuytdorp National Park — wattle (yellow flowers), poverty bush (centre) and the Shark Bay Rose (right).

▲ *Banksia tricuspis*

▲ *Dryandra sessilis*

TOP The Pine Banksia is confined to a small area within Mount Lesueur National Park.

ABOVE Parrot Bush is an unusual plant in that it is almost always in bloom. It flowers profusely in winter and spring, and sporadically throughout the rest of the year.

RIGHT Acorn Banksia is a dominant plant in the coastal heathlands between Cervantes and Dongara and extends to Shark Bay and Perth.

▲ *Banksia prionotes*

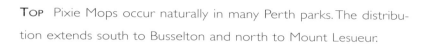

▲ *Petrophile linearis*

▲ *Synaphea spinulosa*

▲ *Dryandra polycephala*

TOP Pixie Mops occur naturally in many Perth parks. The distribution extends south to Busselton and north to Mount Lesueur.

TOP RIGHT Spiny Synaphea is a genus of 15 yellow flowering species, all of them endemic to the southern half of Western Australia.

ABOVE The Showy Dryandra deserves its common name, as it is the most floriferous of all dryandras.

OPPOSITE Shaggy Dryandra flowers were dried by early settlers and used for adorning Christmas trees.

▲ *Dryandra speciosa*

▲ *Verticordia grandis*

▲ *Eucalyptus erythrocorys*

BELOW Rose Mallee is quite rare in the wild as most of its natural habitat between New Norcia and Hill River has been cleared for agriculture. It is widely cultivated for its large and exceptionally handsome flowers.

BOTTOM Geraldton Wax is best known for its profusion of pink, nectar-filled waxy flowers which attract a variety of insects. It is widely cultivated both in Australia and overseas.

▲ *Verticordia nitens*

▲ *Eucalyptus rhodantha*

TOP Illyarrie is a small ornamental tree which is grown for its striking red flower buds that open into bright yellow flowers.

ABOVE Orange Morrison comes into full bloom when most other plants are past their peak, giving a grey-looking banksia woodland understorey a dazzling splash of colour.

OPPOSITE Scarlet Featherflower with its brilliant red flowers and elongated style is one of the most conspicuous wildflowers of the northern heathlands.

▲ *Chamelaucium uncinatum*

◂ Xanthorrhoea p

OPPOSITE The Common Blackboy is a familiar sight in the Mid West and South West. It is a slow-growing tree, adding only 1.5 centimetres to its height each year, thus a three-metre tall Blackboy is about 200 years old.

BELOW Tar Bush is the most widely distributed of all poverty bushes. Its foliage is sticky and the viscous substance can stain the fingers, hence the name.

▼ *Eremophila glabra*

The South West

On the cool, shady realms of the forest region of the South West grows the biggest flowering plant of Western Australia, the magnificent Karri, a smooth, elegant giant reaching to 89 metres. While all tall forests of Western Australia are found in this region, not all forests are as closed and shady as the Karri forests of the extreme south. The Jarrah/Marri forests of the Darling Scarp, for example, are more open and much drier. Further inland, to the north and east, the tall trees form open woodlands rather than forests.

All of the biggest trees in the South West are either eucalypts or bloodwoods, and all belong to the same family, Myrtaceae. Other families are mainly represented by smaller plants. The Protea family, for example, contains two medium-size trees, the Bull and Candle Banksias, and many bushes belonging to at least 10 genera.

Plants of the forest floor are not exposed to the harsh sun for the whole day and have adapted to filtered sunlight passing through the crowns of the forest giants. These plants display great variety of colour and are an absolute delight in springtime. Wattles are plentiful, with a stunning variety of phyllodes, or leaf-like structures, and rather similar yellow flowers.

In contrast to wattles, the plants of the pea family provide an astonishing array of colours. Brown and yellow, as in the Bookleaf Peaflower, are the most common, but other colours abound. Needle-leaved Chorizema brandishes brilliant red flowers, while Devil's Pins and Native Sarsaparilla flowers are deep blue and those of Holly-leaved Mirbelia are pink.

An additional array of wildflowers can be discovered growing around the numerous granite outcrops which are found in these forests. Smaller plants such as orchids, Sundews and Triggerplants are especially abundant, but there are plenty of woody plants growing in close proximity to these outcrops which do not thrive elsewhere. Some of them, like the Granite Petrophile and Granite Featherflower, carry their association with the granite outcrops even in their name.

It is here in the South West where one can see some of the biggest contrasts of the plant kingdom — the miniatures like the Redcoats growing alongside the true giants, the magnificent Karri trees.

▲ *Eucalyptus diversicolor*

ABOVE Karri trees have tall, straight trunks with smooth bark that peels off around February and March each year.
OPPOSITE Karri Dampiera and Holly Flame Pea grow intertwined on the forest floor, sharing the filtered sun.

▲ *Eucalyptus ficifolia*

OPPOSITE Marri is one of the major tall trees of the South West, growing to 60 metres. It belongs to the bloodwoods, a group of eucalypts exuding dark red gum.

LEFT Red-flowering Gum occurs naturally only in a small area of the South West. Because of its striking flowers that vary in colour from light pink to rich red its distribution has been dramatically increased through cultivation.

BELOW Rock Kunzea is a common shrub of the lower parts of the South West, where it grows up to two metres high. The colour of the flowers varies from white to dark pink.

◀ *Corymbia calophylla*   ▲ *Kunzea recurva*

Banksia quercifolia

OPPOSITE An immature Firewood Banksia cone with vertical rows of neatly organised unopened flower buds. The flower opens from the bottom where the mature, pollen-filled anthers form a distinct yellow or orange rim. On top it is usually deep red, patterned with the vertical silver streaks of the unripe flower parts.

ABOVE The Oak-leaved Banksia inhabits swamp edges and wet depressions where it forms a three-metre tall shrub.

LEFT The Candle Banksia flowers from mid-spring to early autumn, attracting honeyeaters and insects at a time of the year when nectar from other sources is dwindling.

Banksia attenuata

Banksia menziesii ▶

OPPOSITE Like the Weeping Wattle, the majority of mature Australian wattles do not have true leaves but phyllodes, which look like leaves but are in reality modified stems.

RIGHT Winged Wattle has no leaves, only flattened (winged) green stems, which are hairy and toothed, with each tooth ending in a sharp thorn.

BELOW Prickly Moses is a very prickly shrub — the thorns prevent large herbivores from eating its nutritious leaves.

▲ *Acacia alata*

◀ *Acacia merinthophora*   ▲ *Acacia pulchella*

▲ *Daviesia incrassata*

LEFT This Daviesia is a nondescript, leafless bush for most of the year. It changes beyond recognition when it bursts into bloom with a profusion of small flowers that cover the whole plant.

BELOW The Globe Pea is a 75 centimetre tall, erect shrub with attractive flowers in all shades between red and yellow which grow on all sides of its leafless stems.

▲ *Sphaerolobium macranthum*

▲ *Macrozamia riedlei*

▲ *Cephalotus follicularis*

▲ *Macrozamia riedlei*

▲ *Cephalotus follicularis*

OPPOSITE TOP LEFT AND OPPOSITE BOTTOM Though superficially looking like palms, Zamias, together with Cycads, belong to a more ancient group of non-flowering plants that preceded the evolution of conifers — true palms, like all other flowering plants, came much later. Zamias have divided sexes with both male and female plants developing cones. After maturing, a female cone releases red seeds to the ground where they germinate a year later.

ABOVE AND OPPOSITE TOP RIGHT The Albany Pitcher Plant is an insectivorous plant which is confined to densely overgrown swamplands between the Donnelly River and Mount Manypeaks. It thrives in nutritionally poor soils by supplementing its nitrogen intake from insects and other arthropods. The pitcher that is used as a trap is a modified leaf. Inside is a liquid in which small creatures drown and decompose before being digested by the plant.

FOLLOWING PAGES Granite outcrops of the South West have thriving populations of sundews, orchids and other small plants, while woody plants form dense thickets around them.

▲ *Pterostylis recurva*

ABOVE The Jug Orchid is the tallest species of a group of orchids known as Greenhoods. It is usually seen sticking out from under various low bushes or among grass stems.

RIGHT The Leopard Orchid is one of 25 West Australian sun orchids, so named because their flowers stay closed at night and during overcast or cold weather.

▲ *Thelymitra benthamiana*

▲ *Drosera menzeisii*

ABOVE One would hardly guess from their fragile flowers that sundews are insectivorous plants. The Pink Rainbow Sundew intertwines its up to one-metre-long stalk into other plants, occasionally using its sticky pads — primarily designed for catching insects — for taking hold. It likes the well-drained soil of high ground.

OPPOSITE Stalked glands that secrete a sticky substance cover the surface of a sundew leaf, modified into an insect-catching organ. Any insect that lands on this leaf is ensnared and, should it try to free itself, more sticky glands attach themselves to its body, gradually immobilising it. The plant then slowly digests its prey with the help of enzymes contained in the sticky liquid.

▲ *Utricularia menziesii*

ABOVE Redcoats are tiny plants found near granite outcrops. They supplement their diet with minute organisms that live in the soil, trapping them into bladders attached to their roots. This whole family is known as Bladderworts.

RIGHT Because of its unique shape and striking colours, the Red and Green Kangaroo Paw has been selected as the Western Australian floral emblem.

▲ *Anigozanthos manglesii*

▲ *Calectasia grandiflora*

Stypandra glauca ▶

▲ *Chamaescilla corymbosa*

LEFT   The Blue Squill is a tiny, shade loving plant. An unusual characteristic of this species is hidden on the underside of its narrow sword-shaped leaves — they are of the same purple colour as the flower petals.

ABOVE   The Blue Tinsel Lily is a perennial plant reaching 50 centimetres in height. The many branched stems are stiff and wire-like, sparsely covered in narrow, prickly leaves and ending in star-shaped, purple flowers adorned by bright yellow anthers.

OPPOSITE   Blind Grass is appropriately named — it is grass-like in outward appearance and some West Australian forms are known to cause blindness in sheep if grazed upon. It grows on rocky outcrops in tussocks similar to some native grasses, however its lily-like flowers that appear in early August immediately give it away.

The South Coast

As one travels further east, yet again the scenery changes. Tall trees gradually disappear, giving way to the windswept heathlands of the South Coast. There is not one particular plant species here that dominates; but rather an overwhelming variety of plants belonging to an incredible array of genera and families. The omnipresent myrtle, protea and pea flower families are represented here by the greatest number of species. Other prominent families are orchids, triggerplants and the Australian heath family.

In the far north-western corner of this region rise the unexpectedly steep peaks of Stirling Range National Park. For any wildflower enthusiast this range would have to be the highlight of the trip. It is the mountain bells that are best known of all Stirling Range flowers. Although some 50 Darwinias occur in other parts of Australia, the nine species of mountain bells that grow here cannot be found anywhere else in the world. Not only that, some peaks of the range have their own species. Bluff Knoll, for instance, has three species, of which the Yellow Mountain Bell that grows on the top does not occur anywhere else in the range.

The Stirling Range National Park is also an excellent place for finding other plants of the region that might be difficult to locate elsewhere. One such a flower that comes immediately to mind is the western equivalent of the Waratah — the Scarlet Banksia, that flowers between June and October, displaying its scarlet flower heads a metre or two above the ground in swampy areas of the park.

The low-laying flats of the South Coast are a playground for orchid lovers, especially in the first spring after fire. Though the flowers of these orchids are tiny when compared with the tropical epiphytic orchids that dangle from rainforest trees, their small size is offset by their profusion. Spider orchids and Little Pink Fan Orchids grow in groups, while Mignonette and Leek Orchids have clusters of flowers on individual stems. The usual colours of the orchids range from white and yellow to pink, but occasionally blue or even red is found.

The South Coast has many florally rich areas beside the Stirling Range. The most outstanding of all is the Fitzgerald River National Park — with its staggering 1784 plant species it is one of the most important national parks in Australia.

Petrophile ericifolia ▶

ABOVE The majority of plants in the southern heathlands belong to the protea and myrtle families.
OPPOSITE Flowers which depend for pollination on nocturnal insects like Flower Scarabs must be visible in the darkness.

▲ *Pimelea physodes*

OPPOSITE The Gillam Bell forms dense thickets on several peaks in the western part of the Stirling Range National Park.

LEFT The Qualup Bell occurs throughout the Fitzgerald River National Park.

BELOW The Blushing Mountain Bell is confined to the Stirling Range from Bluff Knoll to Mount Trio.

◄ *Darwinia oxylepis*   *Darwinia lejostyla* ▲

▲ *Nemcia leakiana*

BELOW LEFT Jacksonia is a genus of about 45 species of peas with characteristically shaped flowers.

LEFT The Mountain Pea is restricted to the upper slopes of the Stirling Range peaks. This image was taken about half way up the Bluff Knoll.

OPPOSITE The Stirling Range Smokebush grows in sand and among rocks in association with taller bushes. It can be found in the Stirling Range and on adjacent sandplains.

BELOW One of two hypocalymmas endemic to Stirling Range, this pink flowering myrtle grows mainly on the lower slopes.

▲ *Jacksonia calycina*

▲ *Hypocalymma speciosum*   *Conospermum dorrienii* ▶

▲ *Banksia coccinea*

LEFT AND ABOVE   The Scarlet Banksia is often mistaken for the Waratah of the eastern seaboard because of its squat red flower heads. However, the resemblance is only super-ficial — although a distant relative, the Waratah belongs to a different genus.

OPPOSITE   The Tennis Ball Banksia is found in three small, isolated areas — the Fitzgerald River National Park, Ravensthorpe Range and in the Wheatbelt, near Hyden.

▲ *Banksia laevigata*

▲ *Caladenia nana*

▲ *Cyanicula sericea*

▲ *Prasophyllum cucullatum*

ABOVE The Hooked Leek Orchid is a small but showy plant which grows along the coast between Albany and Israelite Bay.

TOP RIGHT The Little Pink Fan Orchid is only 15 centimetres high. It grows in groups of five or more plants.

CENTRE RIGHT The Silky Blue Orchid is one of the more common orchids, occurring from Perth to Esperance.

RIGHT Long, ear-like petals gave origin to the common name 'Donkey Orchids' of this group. Depicted here is the Rosy-cheeked Donkey Orchid.

OPPOSITE This photograph of the clump-forming White Spider Orchid was taken in the Stirling Range.

▲ *Diuris porrifolia*   *Caladenia longicauda* ▶

▲   *Hakea laurina*

▲ *Hakea victoria*

LEFT   Because of its beautiful flowers and tidy appearance, the Pincushion Hakea has been cultivated for over 150 years.

ABOVE   The Royal Hakea, with its columnar habit and multi-coloured veined leaves, is a plant unlike any other.

BELOW   The individual flower parts of the Southern Cross are organised into a complex crucifix form.

▲ *Xanthosia rotundifolia*

▲ *Leucopogon cryptanthus*

▲ *Tetratheca hirsuta*

OPPOSITE This Beard Heath is one of over 100 species of plants referred to as Beard Heath found in the south.

ABOVE Black-eyed Susan looks spectacular when flowering en masse, and is common in the Stirling Range.

BELOW The Lilac Hibiscus is an incredibly showy plant which seems out of place in its harsh environment.

LEFT Cow Kicks is a triggerplant with a formidable 'kick', which its column gives to visiting insects.

▲ *Stylidium schoenoides*   ▲ *Alyogyne huegelii*

RIGHT The colours of Starflowers range from white, as seen in this photograph, through to yellow and all shades of pink and red to dark violet.

Calytrix tetragona ▶

The Wheatbelt and Goldfields

People have been attracted to this part of the state for more than a century. First they came in droves to look for gold, the next wave came to wrestle their living from the land as wheat farmers. Although now heavily farmed and mined, this gently undulating country shows its softness every spring, when the hard ground is dotted with millions of delicate wildflowers.

The dominant trees of this region are eucalpts; the Wandoo in the Wheatbelt area, and the Salmon Gum further east in the Goldfields. These woodlands are more open than the Jarrah or Karri forests of the South West, allowing large areas among the fully-grown trees to be bathed in sunlight for most of the day. Shrubs and other woody plants cover most of this well-lit forest floor, but in places patches of annuals form every spring. Daisies, some members of the goodenia family, and trigger-plants, sundews and orchids grow readily in these meadows.

There are other eucalypts growing in this region which form dense communities of slender trees known as mallee wood-lands. Individual species look incredibly alike; they attain the same height, have the same slender eucalypt leaves, the same smooth bark trunks and very similar flowers. The only thing that gives them away to an expert is their nuts, which vary enormously in shape and size. There are, of course, some exceptions, like the Mottlecah, Gungurru and the Pear-fruited Mallee, that have made it into our gardens in a big way precisely because of their different and exceptionally beautiful flowers.

The heathlands in the Wheatbelt are not as extensive as in the Mid West or South Coast regions, but they are also composed of an impressive array of plant species. Myrtles, wattles, peas and fan flowers are all well represented here, the last mentioned mainly by vivid blue species.

However, it is the Family Proteaceae that needs a special mention. Grevilleas, hakeas, coneflowers, synapheas, petrophiles, lambertias, smokebushes and wooly bushes are all richly represented in the Wheatbelt's heathlands. The banksia count is not as high here as elsewhere, but they are replaced by equally stunning Dryandras that are a West Australian specialty and that have reached the peak of their diversity in these heathlands. Flowers of this group are often hidden inside prickly foliage to safeguard their plentiful nectar from unwanted visitors, but to see their beauty is worth of a couple of scratches!

▲ *Gastrolobium micranthum*   *Eucalyptus salmonophloia* ▶

ABOVE Sandplain Poison contains a substance which, while poisonous to livestock, is harmless to native animals.
OPPOSITE The Salmon Gum is one of the most elegant and memorable trees of the state.

▲ *Lechenaultia formosa*

▲ *Dampiera incana*

OPPOSITE AND ABOVE Red Lechenaultia is a popular plant because of its striking colour. This mat-forming variety is the most common in the Wheatbelt region.

LEFT The common name Hairy Dampiera refers to grey hairs that cover this plant's leaves. However, the first thing that strikes any observer is the intense colour of its flowers.

FOLLOWING PAGES Twiggy Dampiera is a perennial herb forming large, dense clumps of vivid flowers — individual clumps look, from a distance, like a blue-coloured balloon.

▲ *Eucalyptus macrocarpa*

▲ *Eucalyptus synandra*

▲ *Eucalyptus occidentalis*

OPPOSITE BOTTOM This Mallee is a rare species from the north-east Goldfields. Unusually long, soft spikes on its flower buds are characteristic of this recently discovered small tree.

OPPOSITE TOP The Mottlecah, with its large silvery leaves and the largest flowers of all eucalypts, can hardly be overlooked here or in the gardens and parks where it is popularly grown.

ABOVE The Swamp Yate is a tree with dark, rough bark on the lower half of its trunk, reminiscent of a sock, and a smooth whitish bark on the upper half.

RIGHT The Gungurru is a very attractive red-flowering small tree, with a reddish-brown trunk and powdery-white new growth and gumnuts. It grows to 10 metres.

▲ *Eucalyptus caesia*

RIGHT AND BELOW Boomerang Triggerplant forms dense mats covering up to a square metre with numerous little flowers facing upwards. Their boomerang-shaped petals give this species its common name.

OPPOSITE A fascinating feature of Triggerplants is their method of pollination. Male and female organs are united into a stigma, which is placed on the end of a long column that is hidden under the plants' petals. The stigma is triggered by an insect landing on a flower — it bounces onto the back of the insect, loading it with pollen or receiving pollen from another plant.

▲ *Stylidium breviscapum*   *Stylidium scandens* ▶

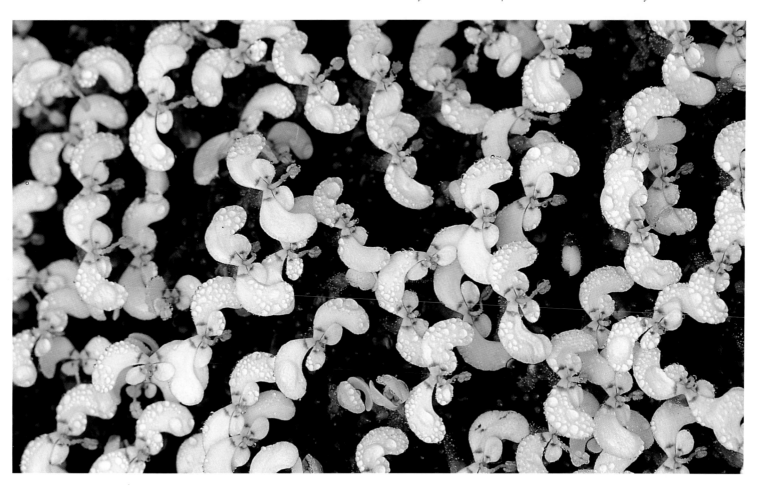

▲ *Petrophile media*   *Grevillea georgeana* ▶

LEFT As the name Nodding Coneflower suggests, the flower heads of this species bend downwards, thus giving the plant in bloom a nodding appearance.

ABOVE This Petrophile shares its place in the sun with blue goodenia and yellow synaphea.

OPPOSITE The stunning red flowers of this grevillea have their devoted admirers even at night. Here the plant is given its chance for cross-pollination by a tiny nocturnal marsupial — the Western Pygmy Possum.

▲ *Isopogon teretifolius*

▲ *Dryandra ferruginea*

LEFT The Rusty Dryandra has the biggest flower head of the genus, reaching seven centimetres in diameter.

BELOW The Honeypot is a prostrate species whose flowers, growing close to the ground, form a cup. It is believed that this shape of flower helps small mammals to reach its nectar.

▲ *Dryandra lindleyana*

The Arid Inland

It is for good reason that this is one of the least populated regions in the world. Summers here are unforgiving, consistently registering the highest temperatures in Australia. Evaporation rates are enormous, and rainfalls meagre and absolutely unreliable. Nevertheless, the flowerless wastes of the Sahara should not be expected — except for the large salt lakes. Even in the dead centre of the deserts, there is a thriving plant life.

To survive these conditions, plants either have to sit out the heat of the summer or perish altogether. Both strategies are employed — the latter by annuals that do not linger any longer than is necessary to give a good start to their progeny. Many species thus survive the harshest part of the year only as seeds.

Other plants have evolved different ways to combat the heat. They usually have small leaves and flowers so that the surface from which water evaporates is reduced. The hairiness of Lambstails, Foxgloves and many other desert plants serve the same purpose. While in the tropics hairiness is used mainly as a protection against grazing animals, here the tufts of hair surrounding the flowers and covering the stems and foliage help to keep water evaporation to a minimum.

No botanical treatise on the arid interior of Western Australia would be complete without Spinifex Grass. To most, the spinifex, with its sharp spines capable of piercing a thick leather boot, is just an obstacle to travel, but for those who learn to accept it, it becomes an inseparable part of the outback beauty. It is also an important habitat for desert creatures that depend for their protection on those frustration-causing spikes.

Any visit to the interior of Western Australia would be unthinkable without seeing a carpet of red Sturt's Desert Peas. It is a short-lived, prostrate plant that has become an Australian icon. The best place to look for Sturt's Desert Peas is near creeks or lakes and in places that retain moisture long after the rains.

This is the largest and most geographically diverse of all Western Australia's wildflower regions. It covers all West Australian deserts, most of the mulga country and numerous inland ranges. It even contains the largest lakes (although they seldom fill with water) and the longest shoreline — on the west coast between Shark Bay and the Kimberley and on the south coast along the Great Australian Bight. Scientifically it is known as the Eremaean Botanical Province.

▲ *Dicrastylis castelloi*　　　　*Newcastelia sp.* ▶

ABOVE AND OPPOSITE Lambstails are so called because of their woolly appearance — their flowers, stems and foliage are covered by dense hair as protection against water loss. Most lambstails are found in the arid regions of Australia.

▲ *Solanum phlomoides*

OPPOSITE Native Tomatoes belong to a large family of about 2300 species, which includes some important vegetables like potato and tomato. The fruit of the species, although resembling a small yellow tomato when mature, is not edible.

LEFT A minature burrowing bee collects pollen from a Native Tomato. Native Tomato flowers are usually purple, blue or white with five yellow stamens in the centre.

BELOW The Flannel Bush is the most common of native tomatoes in the region.

◄ *Solanum phlomoides*

Solanum lasiophyllum ▲

▲ *Thryptomene maisonneuvei*

LEFT AND BELOW The Desert Heath Myrtle has tiny flowers and leaves. The leaves lack stalks and cover the length of the branches. It often assumes the shape of a small tree, as seen below, with a complex root system to keep it firmly anchored in the unstable environment of a sand dune.

OPPOSITE The dry rocky terrain of the inland ranges comes to life after a good rain. Three closely related species — the Mat, Green and Weeping Mulla Mulla are seen here flowering together on a rocky slope.

▲ *Acacia synchronicea*

▲ *Eremophila leucophylla*

▲ *Eremophila latrobei*

ABOVE Desert fuchsias, such as the White-leaved Desert Fuchsia, are endemic to Australia and abundant in arid regions. They are not related to the fuchsias frequently grown in gardens.

OPPOSITE This rare desert wattle is one of about 100 species found in the arid region. It is a prolifically flowering bush growing to over three metres.

ABOVE Warty leaves and vivid red, nodding flowers that appear after rain are the main characteristics of the Warty Fuchsia. It is a hardy plant, found in a variety of arid habitats.

BELOW Poverty bushes and desert fuchsias belong to the same group of plants. This species of poverty bush is distinguished by the three elongated bottom lobes of its flowers.

▲ *Eremophilia sp.*

▲ *Corymbia setosa*

ABOVE A common sight in the arid inland, the Rough-leaved Bloodwood is easily distinguished from other white trunk gum trees by its rough, stalkless, stem-clasping leaves.

LEFT AND BELOW Climbing Morning Glory is a vigorous climber with a profusion of striking, trumpet-shaped flowers. Tubers growing on its root system are good 'bush tucker' when baked and give it its other name — Potato Vine.

▲ *Ipomoea costata*

RIGHT Sturt's Desert Pea is an earth-hugging creeper with clusters of big, brilliantly red flowers with black centres. An Australian icon, it is instantly identifiable around the world.

BELOW The Flame Pea is one of about 650 species of pea flowers found in Western Australia. All members of this particular genus *Tephrosia* have brightly coloured flowers and are either annual or perennial herbs.

▲ *Tephrosia flammea*

▲ *Swainsona formosa*

The Kimberley

The rugged beauty of the West Australian tropics is not for the faint-hearted. Up here it is a real wilderness — the biggest chunk of wilderness left in Australia. As with the rest of the Australian tropics, the climate of the Kimberley region is governed by the monsoon season. The north-west of the region receives a great deal of rain (most years well over 1000 millimetres), most of it falling between November and March. During this wet season the many dirt roads in the region are more often than not impassable. The inland parts of the Kimberley receive much less rain, and consequently the vegetation of the southern fringe is more reminiscent of the adjacent deserts than the rest of the region

The north-west is lush and tropical, with patches of rainforest and creeks lined with impenetrable thickets of Screw Pines. The rainforest here is restricted to small areas, but even these have populations of tree-hugging orchids and epiphytic ferns. It is also here in the north-west Kimberley where Giant Water Lilies with their pink and white flowers cover numerous billabongs and pools.

The most easily recognised tree here is the Boab — a close relative of the African Baobab — with its huge bottle-shaped tree trunk. Early settlers utilised this feature — they dug out the inside of a trunk and used it as a shelter or sometimes, as in the case of the Derby Prison Tree, even as a temporary prison. In times of drought, farmers used to fell the younger Boab trees and slice them open for cattle, because the inside of the trunk is filled with moist and edible pith. The Boab is a deciduous tree shedding its leaves for the dry season. Consequently most visitors to the Kimberley see the Boab only in its dormant state.

There are other winter–deciduous trees that are leafless during the dry season, however some of them utilise the nutrients reabsorbed from the leaves for their propagation. So one can find a dead-looking stump of a tree, half-covered with beautiful flowers. Two small trees that belong to this category are the Sticky Kurrajong and yellow-flowering Kapok Bush.

It is not always easy to find a good range of Kimberley flowers in bloom, however, a visit early in the season rather than later is recommended. Though conditions vary every year, the tourist season starts in late May and by September this region is usually too dry for most plants to flower.

▲ *Nymphaea gigantea*

ABOVE AND OPPOSITE The Giant Water Lily is a beautiful aquatic plant found in tropical lagoons, billabongs and quiet river ponds in northern Australia, including the pictured Bell Gorge in the King Leopold Range.

▲ *Avicennia marina*

▲ *Adansonia gregorii*

OPPOSITE Screw Pines are the main component of vegetation along Kimberley watercourses, where they often form impenetrable thickets.

ABOVE LEFT White mangroves, the most common of the 17 mangrove species found along the West Australian coast, grow in tidal zones where they are regularly bathed in salt water.

ABOVE RIGHT Some Boab trees can attain a girth of 20 metres, while not exceeding a height of 10 metres. The trees can live to over 100 years old.

◄ *Pandanus aquaticus*

RIGHT   The Rock Fig is a familiar sight in northern Australia. Hanging over ledges, it sends down numerous aerial roots and peppers the ground underneath with thousands of fruits.

BELOW   The 'fruits' of the Rock Fig, which many birds and mammals love to eat, are not actual fruits but receptacles — fleshy capsules enveloping male and female flowers.

▲ *Ficus platypoda*

Grevillea refracta

LEFT   The beautiful red and yellow flowers of the Tropical Grevillea are initially held erect before slowly bending down into a typical dangling grevillea position.

OPPOSITE TOP   Sticky Kurrajong is a small winter–deciduous tree found on rocky slopes. It sheds its felted leaves at the onset of the dry season, exchanging them for scarlet blossoms.

OPPOSITE BOTTOM   Crab Eyes is a lovely climber with small pink to violet flowers, but is better known for its bright red and black seeds that are virulently toxic.

BELOW   Carpets of pink-flowering Bachelors Buttons are very attractive to insects. Here the Lesser Wanderer uses its long proboscis for sucking nectar from the flower cup.

Gomphrena canescens

▲ *Sterculia viscidula*

▲ *Abrus precatorius*

▲ *Ipomoea brasiliensis*

▲ *Cochlospermum fraseri*

LEFT Beach Morning Glory can be found on tropical beaches around the world.

ABOVE The Kapok Bush has pleasantly scented yellow flowers and is a common sight throughout the Kimberley.

OPPOSITE A White-gaped Honeyeater feeds on eucalypt blossoms on the Mitchell Plateau, in the north-west Kimberley.

BELOW The Snow-White Tree Orchid is another winter—deciduous plant that is leafless when in flower.

▲ *Dendrobium affine*

▲ *Eucalyptus sp.*

Ptilotus exaltatus

OPPOSITE AND ABOVE Tall Mulla Mulla is the most wide-spread and consequently the best known of all mulla mullas. It is found in all Australian states, except Victoria and Tasmania, and prefers drier habitats, but grows taller and more luxuriant after good soaking rains. Tall Mulla Mullas can often be found alongside roads where they benefit from the additional run-off water.

▲ *Crotalaria cunningamii*

LEFT The Green Birdflower is a sand-loving plant, inhabiting the coast, dry riverbeds and desert sand dunes. Its large, inflated, sausage-shaped pods rattle in the wind when ripe. Plants from this group are commonly called rattlepods.

OPPOSITE The Woolybutt is a small tree, up to 20 metres high, with brilliant orange flowers. Its common name refers to the distinctly dark woolly bark on the lower half of the trunk.

BELOW The flower brushes of the Cadjeput can grow up to 16 centimetres long, and are frequented by hordes of insects, honeyeaters, sugar gliders, and fruit and blossom bats.

▲ *Melaleuca leucadendra*

Eucalyptus miniata ▶

Index

▲ *Waitzia nitida*

Marie and I would like to especially thank our editor Anna Sanders for her invaluable assistance;
Dr Greg Keighery from the West Australian department of CALM for his generous help with
plant identification and Jennifer Sarson for proofreading the manuscript.

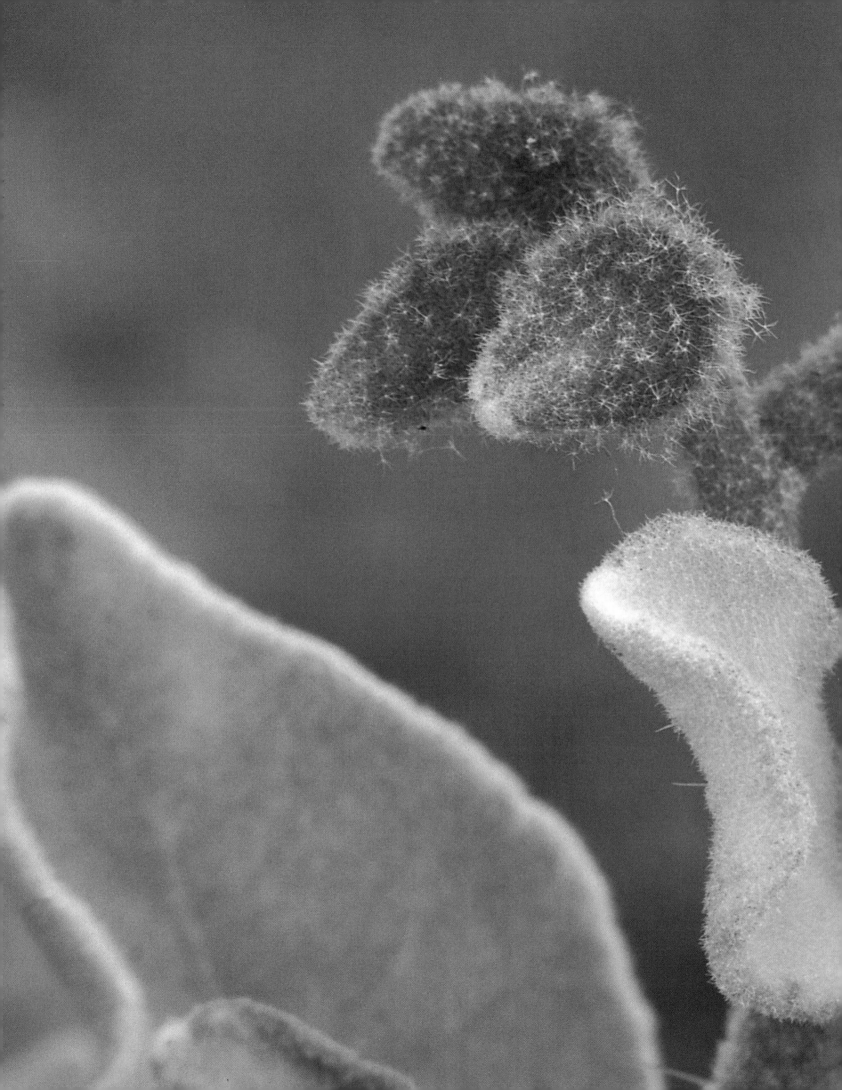